NOW YOU CAN READ ABOUT....

RESCUE FROM DANGER

TEXT BY HARRY STANTON

ILLUSTRATED BY TONY GIBBONS

BRIMAX BOOKS • NEWMARKET • ENGLAND

There has been an accident.
Someone has been hurt.
The ambulance is rushing to
hospital. Can you see the
light flashing on the ambulance?
It is also sounding its siren.

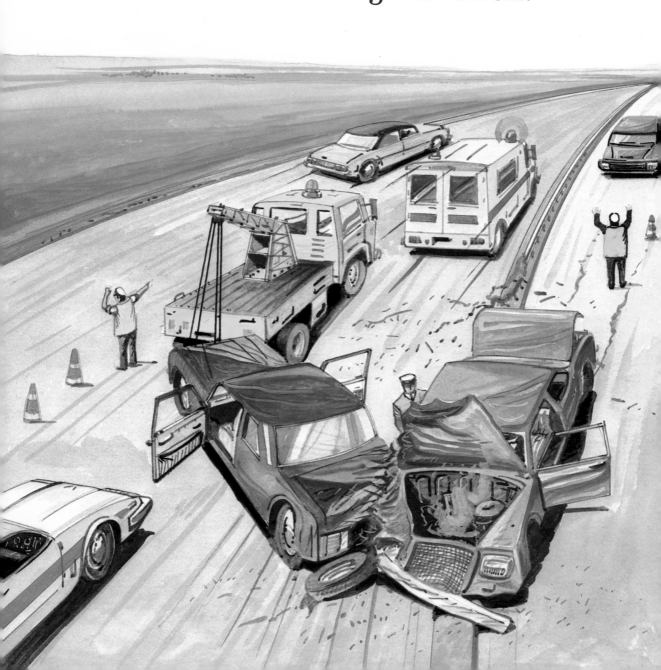

At night the police rescue truck uses its powerful light. Afterwards the light is lowered down into the truck.

The police are helping to rescue people. They are directing the traffic and putting out signs.

This is one of the
first ambulances.
It was used 200
years ago by the
French army. Two
wounded soldiers
could be carried
in the ambulance.

Long ago rowing boats were used
to rescue shipwrecked sailors.

This is one of the first fire
engines. It was pulled by
fire-fighters to the fire.
The hoses were made of leather.
Many people were needed to
work the pumps.

Look at this steam
pump. It was made
nearly 100 years
ago. It was pulled
by horses.

This fire engine can carry ten men.
It has a pump that can spray water
to the top of high buildings.
It also has a large tank of water
used to put out small fires.

Look at the people
at the top of the
building. They are
trapped. The long
ladders are used
to bring them down.

This Ladder Truck is used in
America. When it is driven the back
wheels also have to be steered.

At an airport fire trucks are
always ready. They have very
powerful engines. They can race
along the runway to help an
aircraft that has crashed.

The fire truck carries enough water to fill a small swimming pool. The water is mixed with a chemical to make foam. It is sprayed on to the aircraft to put out fire. The foam also stops a fire starting.

In Australia many farms are hundreds of miles from the nearest doctor. When a person has an accident or becomes ill, the farmer talks to a doctor by radio. The doctor tells him how to care for the patient.

If someone is very ill, the Flying Doctor will visit him by plane. Look at the patient on the stretcher. The Flying Doctor is taking him to hospital.

S.O.S. Someone needs help.
The yacht is sinking. The crew
race to the lifeboat. The boat is
launched within minutes. The
people will soon be rescued.

The ship is sinking. People are lowered into the sea in small boats. Another ship is coming to their rescue. The Captain is always the last person to leave a sinking ship.

A diver is trapped
under the sea.
This tiny submarine
will rescue him.
Only two or three
people can get
into it.

This strange ship puts out fires on oil rigs. Look for the big hoses. Smaller hoses keep the ship cool when it is close to the fire. They spray water on to the sides of the ship.

These tugs are used to put out fires on ships.

Help! Someone is injured and cannot move. A helicopter has come to the rescue. The pilot is keeping the helicopter steady. They are lowering one of the crew on to the mountain. The injured man will be lifted up into the helicopter.

What rescue machines might we see in the future?

Space shuttles are used to repair satellites. Perhaps one day a space shuttle will be used to rescue astronauts.

Will we see robot fire-fighters? They may be able to go very close to the fires.

Look at this machine. Perhaps it could rescue trapped miners.

One day rescue teams may wear special back packs. Then they could fly to rescue people from danger.

All these rescue machines are in this book. Can you name them?